Nicholas Murray Butler

The Effect of War of 1812

Upon the consolidation of the union

Nicholas Murray Butler

The Effect of War of 1812
Upon the consolidation of the union

ISBN/EAN: 9783337115531

Printed in Europe, USA, Canada, Australia, Japan

Cover: Foto ©ninafisch / pixelio.de

More available books at **www.hansebooks.com**

VII

The Effect of the War of 1812

Consolidation of the Union

JOHNS HOPKINS UNIVERSITY STUDIES

IN

HISTORICAL AND POLITICAL SCIENCE

HERBERT B. ADAMS, Editor

History is past Politics and Politics present History — *Freeman*

FIFTH SERIES

VII

The Effect of the War of 1812

UPON THE

CONSOLIDATION OF THE UNION

By NICHOLAS MURRAY BUTLER, Ph. D.

Tutor in Philosophy in Columbia College
President of the Industrial Education Association's College for the Training of Teachers

PUBLICATION AGENCY OF THE JOHNS HOPKINS UNIVERSITY

JULY, 1887

JOHN MURPHY & CO., PRINTERS
BALTIMORE.

THE EFFECT OF THE WAR OF 1812

UPON THE

CONSOLIDATION OF THE UNION.

The two great motive forces in American politics during the first century of the national existence were the questions of state sovereignty and of slavery. The pressure of the first was almost wholly, yet but temporarily, relieved by the second war with Great Britain, and it was reserved for the great civil war of 1861–5 to put an effectual quietus upon both.

The course of the conflict over these questions shows that until the war of 1812 that of state sovereignty, pure and simple, occupied the foremost place in the nation's political activity. From the conclusion of that war period until 1861 the question of slavery, with all its far-reaching collateral issues, asserted its preëminence, and in its disastrous overthrow and complete downfall carried the state sovereignty heresy with it to a common ruin.

The concrete question with which we are to deal at present is the effect of the war of 1812 on the consolidation of the Union. To understand this intelligently we must acquaint ourselves with the positions taken in reference to the state-sovereignty dispute down to the time when war was declared, and with the condition of the Union at that time in respect to real unity. We must examine the political character and motives of the war itself, and discover the status of the

5

national unity in the years immediately succeeding the war. When all this is done we shall be entitled to pronounce upon the effect of the war of 1812 on the consolidation of the Union.

It is probable that in the light of historical fact, and the full discussion which the question has since received, culminating in the irrevocable verdict of a terrible civil war, no one will care to deny that the Declaration of Independence of July 4th, 1776, was the act of an ethnographically and geographically unified nation, and not the separate though synchronous deed of thirteen constituent parts of that nation. Moreover, the authority of the Continental Congress as a revolutionary body cannot be questioned. It was this Congress that drew up and adopted the Articles of Confederation of 1781. But even at the time of the original adoption of these Articles by Congress, November 14th, 1777, the enthusiasm of 1776 was abated; the national ardor had cooled and had been superseded by more particularistic and selfish feelings. Thus the infant nation of 1776, even before it had risen from its cradle, seemed sickening to its death.

"The preponderance of the anti-national tendencies during the early life of the Union undoubtedly had its origin in the political and social development of the states, in their want of political connection before the Revolution, in the little intercourse, commercial and other, between them, and lastly in various differences in their natural situation which rendered a rapid intergrowth of the several States impossible and the collisions attendant thereon unavoidable."[1]

When the time came to form a national government it was but natural that two opposing views should be taken as to the extent of the powers to be conferred upon that government.

To begin with, the very nature of the question provoked, if it did not require, the formation of two opposing parties;

---

[1] Von Holst, The Constitutional and Political History of the United States, Chicago, 1877, Vol. I. pp. 106, 107.

then, the selfish feelings of a particular state or states, loth
to give up natural advantages to the common weal, would
oppose a strong central government, and in any such movement as the American Revolution, an ultra-democratic party,
large or small as the case may be, is sure to develop. But in
this case fact proved more powerful than theory. The stern
necessities of the case and the ably-defended opinions of Hamilton, Madison, and their coadjutors, in spite of the technical
provisions of the Articles of Confederation, carried through
the proposition for the Philadelphia Convention of 1787, and
in it sounder political science prevailed. As a result our
present Constitution was promulgated.

The great Constitutional Party, as we may appropriately
describe the Federalists, immediately after the organization
of the government under the instrument of 1787, put forth
by word and deed a theory of government deduced from
their interpretation of the Constitution, which in reality they
had framed. The occasion of the crystallization of the elements of this party into an unified whole was the struggle for
the adoption and adjustment of the system of 1787. Their
theory was, in brief, that the government was based on a
national popular sovereignty, that the central government
should be independent in all its machinery of the local governments, exercising all general powers and interpreting by
its own constituted agents what was local and what was general, under such limitations as were put upon it in the Constitution itself by the national popular sovereignty. But in
the struggle this party was obliged to give up, if indeed it
ever distinctly held, a wholly national doctrine and ground
itself for the purpose of victory on a federal system, midway
between confederation and nationalism, though strongly lean-
ing toward the latter. This federal system, though still hold-
ing to the sovereignty of the people of the United States as
ultimate, yet admitted that a system of local commonwealth
governments was fundamental in our political system. In
other words, it allowed that the Union was one of states, but
not of state governments.

The original opponents of this doctrine cannot be dignified
with the name party. Their nucleus was a few extremists of
the Rousseau stamp, who believed or pretended to believe that
the state of nature was the only perfect state and that all
society had originated in a social compact; that government,
which is in its very nature tyrannical and oppressive, had
grown up from an exaggeration of powers originally relin-
quished by the individual in the compact. Around such men
and opinions as these the opposition to Federalism began to
collect. It acquired strength and definiteness by the debates
on the Funding[1] and Assumption[2] bills, the Slavery Peti-
tion[3] debate of 1790, the Excise Tax,[4] the National Bank
bill,[5] and from the complications in foreign affairs in which
the administration became involved. In addition "the French
Revolution introduced from abroad an element which, independent of the actual condition of affairs and partly in conflict
with it, kept excitement at the boiling point during many
years.[6] The French Revolution was at first hailed with delight
by all parties in the United States; when, however, after the
death of Mirabeau, the impossibility of control and the mis-
takes of the helpless court transferred the preponderance of
power to the radicals and when the anarchical elements daily
grew bolder, the Federalists began to turn away. The anti-

---

[1] Von Holst, I. 85, 86. Hildreth, History of the United States of America.
New York, Harper and Brothers, 1851, Vol. IV. 152-171, 213-220. This and
most of the following references to Hildreth are given to show where fuller
information on the subjects referred to may be found.

[2] Hildreth, IV. 171-174, 213-220.

[3] Von Holst, I. 89-93; Hildreth, IV. 174-204. In this debate the threat
of civil war was uttered on the floor of the House of Representatives for
perhaps the first time. The speaker was Tucker of South Carolina, and his
words were: "Do these men expect a general emancipation by law? This
would never be submitted to by the Southern States without a civil war."
See Benton, Abridgment of the Debates of Congress, I. 208.

[4] Von Holst, I. 94, 95; Hildreth, IV. 253-256.

[5] Von Holst, I. 104-106; Hildreth, IV. 256-267.

[6] Hildreth, IV. 411-413.

Federalists on the other hand clung more dearly to it than ever. The farther France proceeded, by the adoption of brutal measures, in the direction of political idealism, the more rank was the growth in the United States of the most radical doctrinarianism; the more attentively the legislators of France listened to Danton's voice of thunder and Marat's fierce cry for blood, the more boldly did demagogism in its most repulsive form rage in the United States." [1]

Many of the objections to the Federalist measures were closely bordering on the ridiculous, while but a few were defensible. " But no reasoning was too absurd to find credulous hearers when the rights of the States were alleged to be in danger and the services of the phantom 'consolidation' were required. The politicians would not, however, in a, matter of such importance have dared to wage so strong a war of opposition and they could not have carried it on for ten years and have finally conquered, if they had not had as a broad and firm foundation to build upon, the anti-nationalistic tendencies which prevailed among the people." [2]

The word anti-nationalistic is used advisedly; for by it is meant that among the people there was a strong feeling that any dissatisfied state or number of states might secede or withdraw at pleasure from the Union. Nor was this idea by any means confined to the anti-Federalists or to that section of the country in which their strength mainly lay. It is also a mistake to suppose that these feelings never found vent in words until the great slavery contest, many years later. In point of fact, as early as 1793, when peace with England was endangered by Genet's machinations and their consequences, there were those in the New England States who in no covert language urged that a dissolution of the Union was preferable to war with Great Britain. Here are the words of Th. Dwight,

---

[1] Von Holst, I. 107.
[2] Von Holst, I. 106.
[3] Von Holst, I. 112–118; Hildreth, IV. 412–440, 477, 478.

writing at this time to Wolcott: "A war with Great Britain, we, at least in New England, will not enter into. Sooner would ninety-nine out of one hundred of our inhabitants separate from the Union than plunge themselves into an abyss of misery."[1] Hence it is evident that the geographical grouping of the friends and enemies of the Jay treaty[2] did not escape them in spite of appearances which were at first deceptive. Going beyond the limits of the question immediately under consideration they pointed to a division of the republic into two great sections and declared an understanding between them to be a condition precedent to the continuation of the Union. Wolcott writes to his father the following, August 10th, 1795: "I am, however, almost discouraged with respect to the southern states; the effect of the slave system has been such that I fear our government will never operate with efficacy. . . . . Indeed we must of necessity soon come to a sober explanation with the people and know upon what we are to depend."[3]

It was reserved for the Alien and Sedition laws of 1798[4] to call forth from the opposition their first definite declaration of political principles. This is contained in the Kentucky and Virginia Resolutions and in the supplements thereto passed on receipt of the replies from other State Legislatures. But we find another instance of definite talk concerning disruption before these resolutions were passed. In May of 1798, the idea of separation arose in the South as a means of escape from the supremacy of Massachusetts and Connecticut, which had to the Southern States become unbearable. John Taylor of Virginia, by no means an unimportant man, said "it was not unwise now to estimate the separate mass of Virginia and North Carolina with a view to their separate existence."[5] Jefferson wrote him in relation to this matter, June 1st, 1798,

---

[1] Gibbs, Mem. of Walcott, 1. 107. Quoted by Von Holst.
[2] Von Holst, I. 122–128; Hildreth, IV. 488, 539–556, 590–616.
[3] Gibbs, Mem. of Walcott, 1. 224.
[4] Von Holst, I. 142; Hildreth, V. 216, 225–228.
[5] Von Holst, 1. 143.

that it would not be wise to proceed immediately to a disruption of the Union when party passion was at such a
height.[1]

The Kentucky Resolutions[2] of November 10th, 1798, and
November 14th, 1799, really sounded the keynote of the
Federalists' opponents, who had now come to be called Republicans. In brief their position was that the Constitution
was a compact to which the states were integral parties, and
that each party had an equal right to judge for itself as well
of infractions of that compact as of the mode and measures
of redress; and that the rightful remedy against the oppres-
sion of the central government or the exercise by it of any
ungranted powers, was the nullification of any obnoxious act
by the state or states objecting thereto. This was distinct
and exact as far as it went, but it left to Calhoun and a greater
crisis the logical pursuance of the doctrines to their farthest
conclusions.

If the claim to the right of nullification as set forth in 1799
was well-grounded, the Constitution was indeed different from
the Articles of Confederation in particulars, but the political
character of the Union was essentially unchanged, and it was
now as before, a confederation of the loosest structure. On
this very point the comment has been well made: "to the
extent that practice was in accord with theory a mere mechanical motion would have taken the place of organic life. Sooner
or later even that would have ceased, for the state is an organism, not a machine."[3]

Washington now, December 25th, 1798, in writing to
Lafayette, declared that "the Constitution, according to their
[the anti-Federalists'] interpretation of it, would be a mere
cipher."[4] Three weeks later he wrote to Patrick Henry:

---

[1] Jefferson, Works, IV. 245-248.
[2] Von Holst, I. 144-155; Hildreth, V. 272-277, 296, 319-321.
[3] Von Holst, I. 151, 152.
[4] Washington, Works, XI. 378.

"Measures are systematically and pertinaciously pursued which must eventually dissolve the Union or produce coercion."[1]

Very shortly afterward the ultimate consequences of the Kentucky interpretation of the Constitution were boldly drawn.[2] Tucker, whose edition of Blackstone appeared in 1803, writes: "The Federal government, then, appears to be the organ through which the united republics communicate with foreign nations and with each other. Their submission to its operation is voluntary; its councils, its engagements, its authority are theirs, modified and united. Its sovereignty is an emanation from theirs, not a flame in which they have been consumed, nor a vortex in which they have been swallowed up. Each is still a perfect state, still sovereign, still independent and still capable, should the occasion require, to resume the exercise of its functions in the most unlimited extent."[3] Surely there is little here that marks any degree of consolidation. This makes the Constitution but a bond of straw and the nation to be no nation; nothing but a mere conglomeration of independent commonwealths. And when we recollect that this view was that of a large majority of the people at that time, and then read anew the Constitution and its exposition as given by its framers, we must agree with John Quincy Adams in saying that "the Constitution itself had been extorted from the grinding necessity of a reluctant nation."[4]

The hold of the Federalists, which had gradually been growing weaker, was effectually loosened once and forever by the presidential election of 1800. Up to that time that party

---

[1] Washington, Works, XI. 389.

[2] Von Holst, I. 151, note.

[3] Tucker's Blackstone, Philadelphia, 1803, I., Part 1, Appendix, p. 187.

[4] The Jubilee of the Constitution, a discourse delivered at the request of the New York Historical Society on Tuesday, the 30th of April, 1839, being the fiftieth anniversary of the inauguration of George Washington as President of the United States, New York, 1839, p. 55.

had controlled the executive, the judiciary, and the Senate, although the House of Representatives had on several occasions contained an opposition majority. The accession of Jefferson to power was the death-knell of the Federalist party, and from 1800 until their final dissolution they were an ineffective and vacillating minority.

The downfall of the Federalist party explains in a great measure the security which the continuance of the Union enjoyed during the two following decades.[1] The party which represented particularistic and nullifying tendencies was in power and had an overwhelming majority, both legislative and popular, behind it. But although the possibility of a disruption was thus very small, yet the essence of the internal struggle remained the same. Indeed its character was placed in a clearer light by the facts that the parts played by each party were changed, so far as the question of right was concerned, and that the opposition, in spite of its weakness, was not satisfied with wishes and threats of separation, but began in earnest to devise plans of dissolution.

These mutterings were first heard in connection with the purchase of Louisiana in 1803.[2] The New England states especially opposed its consummation as affording to the southern states a source of power with which to become predominant in the Union for all future time; and they feared that the incorporation of the western territory into the Union and its economic development would prove injurious to their own commerce.

These two elements together had weight enough to draw from them the declaration that they would be forced to a separation from the Union. Plumer of New Hampshire declared in the Senate: "Admit this western world into the Union, and you destroy at once the weight and importance of the eastern states, and compel them to establish a separate

---

[1] Hildreth, V. 414–418.
[2] Von Holst, I. 183–187; Hildreth, V. 478–481.

independent empire." [1] And also Griswold of Connecticut, the acknowledged leader of the Federalists, declared in the House, October 25th, 1803: "The vast unmanageable extent which the accession of Louisiana will give to the United States, the consequent dispersion of our population, and the distribution of the balance which it is so important to maintain between the eastern and the western states, threatens at no very distant day, the subversion of our Union." [2] And although chronologically out of place, it will not be amiss to recall the speech of Josiah Quincy, delivered in the House of Representatives, January 14th, 1811, on the bill "To enable the People of the Territory of Orleans to form a Constitution and state Government, and for the admission of such state into the Union." [3] Mr. Quincy did not hold that a state had either a constitutional or a natural right to withdraw from the Union when it thought such a course best for its own interests; but he did maintain that such a violation of the fundamental compact might be made that the moral obligation to maintain it ceased and the right of revolution attached. His words are: "—I am compelled to declare it as my deliberate opinion that, if this bill passes, the bonds of this Union are virtually dissolved; that the states which compose it are free from their moral obligations: and that as it will be the right of all, so it will be the duty of some, to prepare definitely for a separation amicably, if they can; violently, if they must. . . . Suppose, in private life, thirteen form a partnership and ten of them undertake to admit a new partner without the concurrence of the other three, would it not be at their option to abandon the partnership after so palpable infringement of their rights? How much more in political partnership, where the admission of new associates, without previous authority, is so pregnant with obvious dangers and evils. . . . This bill,

---

[1] Von Holst, I. 187, note.
[2] Von Holst, I. 187, note.
[3] Hildreth, VI. 266.

if it passes, is a death-blow to the Constitution. It may afterwards linger; but lingering, its fate will, at no very distant period be consummated." [1]

Recollecting the date at which this speech was delivered, it will be noticed that it is of very great importance in connection with our subject, as showing that just previous to the outbreak of the war with Great Britain, such opinions, marking no real consolidation in the Union, were openly expressed on the floor of the National Legislature.

The statement not infrequently made, that at the time of the Louisiana purchase there were no serious thoughts of a disruption of the Union is untrue. In the letters of the Federalists we find not only that wishes to that end were expressed, but that formal plans were devised. It is admitted that they had no prospect of success; yet the fact that they were so seriously discussed is another link in the chain of cumulative evidence to prove that the Union, so-called, was really no Union at all. [2]

Later, in 1806, when it seemed as if the north and the south had begun to close the breach between them, came the embargo question to tear open the old sores and create new ones. [3] And in this case, at least, the opposition acted not from sentiment alone, for the embargo touched the pockets of a great part of the country. "The planters' staple articles, principally tobacco and cotton, remained unsold, but the planters themselves suffered relatively but little damage. Their products would keep and they were sure of finding a market again as soon as the harbors were open. The farmers sold a considerable portion of their products in the country itself, but the rest was a total loss. The productive industry of the New England fishermen,

---

[1] An abstract of this celebrated speech and an account of the circumstances attending its delivery will be found in the "Life of Josiah Quincy," by his son, Edmund Quincy, Boston, 1867. Pp. 205-218.
[2] Von Holst, I. 193-199.
[3] Von Holst, I. 201-217.

ship-builders, ship-owners, importers and exporters, and all who were dependent on them, ceased almost entirely."[1]

"In this dispute also it is impossible not to recognize a division of parties arising from diverse interests produced by geographical position, and every struggle in which this played any part became in consequence doubly bitter. The South, which held the balance of power in the reigning party and so was primarily responsible for the embargo, would have least to suffer from it. The powerless minority of the New England states, the consideration of whose interests, it was pretended, dictated the measures of the administration, had greatest cause for complaint. The middle states occupied a position betokened by their name; their interests unquestionably inclined them more toward the North, but they wavered from one side to the other."[2] Nowhere here do we see any disposition to consult each other's interests as if the good of one were the advantage of the whole. No such advanced idea of the national unity then existed.

The investigation of the information bought by Madison from the British spy, Henry,[3] discloses still further the fact that at this time secession was regarded as the panacea for all real or fancied oppressions. Henry's mission confessedly was to find out and report to his chief, Sir James Craig, Governor of Canada, how far the Federalists would feel inclined to look to England for support in case of a disruption of the Union. One of the most distinguished sons of Massachusetts was of opinion that Henry would find support enough for his operations, if the Administration's policy was not changed. As early as November, 1808, John Quincy Adams expressed the fear that this might lead to civil war. Later he claimed to have unequivocal evidence to prove that there was a systematic

---

[1] Von Holst, I. 209. Cf. Benton, Ab. Debates of Congress, III. 692; IV, 64.

[2] Von Holst, I. 209, 210.

[3] Von Holst, I. 221, 222; Hildreth, VI. 234-237, 390.

attempt making to dissolve the Union. In his opinion New
England would have undoubtedly made sure of the assistance
of Great Britain if the Administration had made civil war
inevitable by an effort to overcome the resistance to the
embargo by force or by extending it farther.[1]

In this hasty glance at the salient points in the history of
the country from 1789 to 1811, in so far as it bears upon our
subject, we find nationalization nowhere, decentralization everywhere. Secession, so far from being regarded as unconstitu-
tional or unjustifiable under any circumstances, was the club
with which every minority on any important question strove
to beat the majority to terms. It mattered not what opinions
as to ultimate sovereignty the parties held. Such considera-
tions as this were lost sight of in the strifes of sectional preju-
dices and the clash of material interests. "Judged from an
impartial standpoint, the fact that the possibility of civil war
or a division of the Union were so frequently and on relatively
insignificant occasions, thought of on both sides, may be fairly
taken as a measure of the degree of consolidation which the
Union had attained at that time. The actual condition of
affairs presented so unusual a complication of positive and
negative factors so peculiarly grouped, that it was no easy
matter to determine their sum total."[2] It is interesting to
read here the following words, uttered in 1828 :[3] "It is a
melancholy reflection—a subject that excites our best and
inmost feelings—that projects or speculations as to a dissolution have been so frequently indulged. That leading men in
Virginia looked to a dismemberment in 1798-9, when the
armory was built; that Burr and his confederates had an eye
to the establishment of a western government in 1805-6; that
many contemplated a building up of the 'Nation of New
England' from 1808 to 1815, seems to us undoubted; but

---

[1] Von Holst, I. 222, 223.
[2] Von Holst, I. 220, 221.
[3] See Niles' Register, XXXV. p. 210.

2

the lengths to which either party proceeded rest very much on
conjecture or depend on opinion. . . . But whatever have
been the designs of individuals, we have always believed that
the vast body of the people have ever been warmly attached to
the Union." In view of our discussion the last sentiment,
however desirable, certainly seems unwarranted, and at the
declaration of war in June of 1812 we have the spectacle of a
government composed of eighteen[1] sovereign integers, each
looking to its own interest alone, never consulting the general
weal, and claiming the right and the duty to secede from the
so-called Union whenever such a course might seem most
favorable to its individual interests. What effect the war with
Great Britain was to have upon the consolidation of the Union,
we can now understandingly inquire.

Into a detailed account of the course of events abroad which
brought about the war of 1812 we must not here enter. But
we must examine the causes and character of the war in so far
as they have a direct bearing upon parties and sections in the
United States.

The beginning of 1808 saw the Berlin and Milan decrees of
Napoleon and the Orders in Council of England all in force,[2]
and Jefferson, his second term nearing its close, at the helm of
state in the United States. To his Administration five courses
of action were open, some one of which must be adopted as its
own and worked out to its logical conclusion. This choice
lay between (1) doing nothing and allowing the individual
ship-owners to help themselves as best they might; or (2)
attempting a further negotiation with England; or (3) sus-
pending all commerce with the outside world; or (4) granting

---

[1] In addition to the original thirteen states the following had been admitted into the Union: Vermont, March 4th, 1791; Kentucky, June 1st, 1792;
Tennessee, June 1st, 1796; Ohio, November 29th, 1802; Louisiana, April
8th, 1812.

[2] Hildreth, VI. 32–35. The Berlin decree was dated November 21st, 1806,
and the Milan decree, December 17th, 1807. The Orders in Council were
of the date of May 16th, 1806 and November 11th, 1807, respectively.

letters of marque and reprisal to American ship-owners; or
(5) declaring war upon England immediately. Of these possible lines of policy, entrance upon the fourth or fifth was
precluded, for a time at least, by a wholesome fear of the
British navy; the first was shut off by a feeling for the
national honor; the third was the choice of the Administration;
but the second had recommended itself as the most natural
and as having precedents in the country's history. Indeed it
had been tried, resulting in the treaty which was agreed upon
in December, 1806, but to which Jefferson had refused his
assent without ever submitting it to the Senate. This step
having thus failed, the Administration had been free to pursue
its chosen policy, and to the Tenth Congress, October 26th,
1807, the President recommended an embargo.[1] His recommendation was dutifully accepted by his party followers in
Congress, and the embargo became a law before the end of the
year. The Federalists upon whose New England constitu-
encies the measure bore heaviest, opposed the measure both on
economic and on constitutional grounds, and their discussion
of this question presents us with what was destined to be but
one of many mortifying exhibitions of the old party of the
Constitution. But on the constitutional objection it was over-
matched and was forced to fall back to the vantage ground of
the economic argument. And this in turn was little heeded
by the party in power, so long as it did not come directly home
to themselves. But when it began to touch their own pockets,
as it did a few months later, then human nature proved to be
too strong for party sentiment.[2] So evident did this become
that Nicholas, of Virginia, the Administration leader on the
floor of the House of Representatives, himself introduced,
January 25th, 1809, a resolution favoring the repeal of the
embargo and the defence of our maritime rights against all
belligerents.[3] After some haggling as to the date on which

---

[1] Hildreth, VI. 55, 56.
[2] Hildreth, VI. 96-106.
[3] Von Holst, I. 214; Hildreth, VI. 125-130.

the Embargo Act should expire, March 15th, 1809, was agreed upon as a compromise and the resolutions were passed. This virtually threw the United States back to the position in which it was when confronted by five possible courses of action, while two of the five,—those by further negotiation and cutting off all intercourse with the outside world—proved useless by the failure of the treaty and of the embargo. The prospect of an amicable solution of the difficulty by a further treaty was poor indeed, if we consider the spirit of the British Government and the hostility of the Republican party to everything British. In Great Britain Mr. Fox was dead and a new Administration had come into power strongly retrograde in policy and having George Canning for its soul. Great Britain was determined to recover her commerce and to take back her seamen, and the United States had no alternative but to submit or fight. The resumption of commerce and its defence, referred to in the Nicholas resolutions, must then be by war.

The Eleventh Congress at its first session voted the continuance of the non-intercourse Act with Great Britain, and then two years passed during which the latter continued the execution of her offensive orders and decrees against neutral commerce. But when the Twelfth Congress assembled in November, 1811, it was felt that some decisive action would soon be taken.[1] The leadership of the dominant party had been assumed by younger and more impetuous men; and with Clay as Speaker of the House, Calhoun standing second on the Committee on Foreign Affairs, and Crawford and Grundy acting with them, war was certain within the year.[2]

The move was quick and emphatic. On November 29th Calhoun's committee reported a resolution declaring "Forbearance has ceased to be a virtue. . . . The period has arrived when in the opinion of your committee it is the sacred

---

[1] For the personal and party constitution of the Twelfth Congress, see Hildreth, VI. 259, 260.
[2] Von Holst, I. 226.

duty of Congress to call forth the resources and patriotism of
the country."[1] In addition the committee recommended that
the standing army be increased by 10,000 men and that the
President be authorized to call 50,000 volunteers under arms.
This was all acceded to without any delay by an overwhelming majority.

But such resolutions were inoperative without the coöperation of the President, and he was for peace. Fortune, however, favored the war party. A presidential election would
take place in the following autumn and Madison was anxious
for a second term. In this the leaders of the war faction saw
their opportunity. They waited upon Madison and plainly
told him that the condition *sine quâ non* of their support in
the coming campaign was his acceptance of their war policy.
Madison knew very well that both Monroe and Gerry were
ready and willing to accept the presidential nomination on a
war platform. This determined his action, and he gave in
his adherence to the war party.[2]

On April 3rd he wrote to Jefferson that the action of the
British government in refusing to repeal the Orders in Council
had left the United States no option but to prepare for war, and
that an embargo of sixty days duration had been recommended.[3]
This recommendation had already been sent in on April 1st. It
was acted upon by Congress, but the war party could not wait.
They drove Madison on, and on June 1st he sent in his message recommending a declaration of war.[4] Two days afterward Calhoun reported on it from his committee, and the
declaration was carried in the House by a vote of 79 to 49.
The Senate was more deliberate, and after two weeks' delay it
passed the declaration, June 17th, by a vote of 17 to 13.

An analysis of this vote is interesting as showing the sectional character of the war party and of the opposition to it.

---

[1] Von Holst, I. 226–227; Hildreth, VI. 262–265.
[2] Von Holst, I. 230–232; Hildreth, VI. 289–291.
[3] Hildreth, VI, 291–294.
[4] Von Holst, I. 232, 233; Hildreth, VI. 303–306.

Louisiana, making the eighteenth state, had just been admitted,
and the House contained 177 members apportioned in the ratio
of one to every thirty-five thousand inhabitants. There were
36 members of the Senate, thus making a total of 213 in both
houses, not including the Vice-President who was presiding
in the Senate. The New York delegation of 27 was then for
the first time more numerous than that of every other state.
Pennsylvania was second with 23 members, and Virginia
third with 22. The members from New Hampshire, most
of those from Massachusetts (which then included what is
now the state of Maine), those from Connecticut, Rhode
Island, New Jersey and Delaware, with several from New
York, some from Virginia and North Carolina, one from
Pennsylvania and three from Maryland, opposed the war.
The members from Vermont, some from New York, all but
one from Pennsylvania, most of them from Maryland, Vir-
ginia and North Carolina, all from South Carolina, Georgia,
Kentucky, Tennessee, Ohio, and Louisiana, supported it.
New Hampshire, Connecticut, Rhode Island, New York,
and Delaware were represented by senators who opposed
the war. Massachusetts and Maryland were divided, while
Vermont, Pennsylvania, Virginia, North Carolina, South
Carolina, Georgia, Kentucky, Tennessee, Ohio, and Louisiana were represented by senators who supported the war.
Of the large sea-board cities, Boston and New York were
represented by members found in the minority. The dele-
gations from Philadelphia, Baltimore, Charleston, and New
Orleans were with the majority. The eastern states as a
rule opposed the war; the western states were all for it,
with the southern and middle states divided. The practical
feature was that the war administration could command a
majority of nearly forty votes in the House and one of four
or five votes in the Senate.

Taking the reasoning portion of the community as the judge,
probably the declaration of war was mostly condemned; but the
instinctive patriotism of the young men of the country enthusias-

tically maintained it. Few denied that sufficient cause for the war existed, but the time and mode of its declaration were condemned. Defensive though the war appeared to be, yet it was offensive in that it was voluntarily undertaken by the United States to compel Great Britain by the invasion and conquest of her North American dependencies, to respect our maritime rights as neutrals.

A united sentiment on the part of the people, more especially those from whom men and money must principally be drawn, would have excused in a great measure the haste and lack of preparation with which the war had been declared and would soon have filled up the ranks of the army and the coffers of the treasury. But any such unanimity was entirely wanting. The policy of the old Republicans, with the exception of the small class of Francomaniacs, as well as of the Federalists, had been alike neutrality and peace. But however peaceful might have been the intentions of Jefferson and his close followers, there had always been a faction, more or less large, which was determined to bring about a war with Great Britain. This faction had served as the nucleus about which various forces and tendencies had caused the now triumphant war party to crystallize.

But that the war was a party one was too evident to be denied even by its warmest advocates. In the first place we have the important address to their constituents by thirty-four members of the minority in the House of Representatives.[1] This address held, in substance, that the United States was a nation (*sic*) composed of eighteen independent sovereignties united by a moral obligation only. It went on to say : " — above all, it appeared to the undersigned from signs not to be mistaken, that if we entered upon this war, we did it as a divided people ; not only from a sense of the inadequacy of our means to success, but from moral and political objections of great weight and very general influence." These " moral and political objections " were con-

---

[1] Niles' Register, II. 369–315.

sidered by the authors of the address to have the greatest
weight, and to their words the next presidential election gave
a peculiar emphasis. The war was the live issue of the campaign and the result showed more plainly than had been done
in many years before, the geographical separation of parties.
All the New England states excepting Vermont, together
with New York, New Jersey and Delaware cast their electoral vote solidly for De Witt Clinton. Maryland was
divided, while Pennsylvania and all the southern and western states voted unanimously for Madison.[1] Aside from
what such a separation as this too plainly indicates, the
proof that the war was a sectional one is cumulative. Six
months before the declaration was made, Macon of North
Carolina, one of the most distinguished of the war party,
said : "And here, sir, permit me to say that I hope this is
to be no party war, but a national war. . . . Such a war,
if war we shall have, can alone, in my judgment, obtain the
end for which we mean to contend, without any disgrace."[2]
And two years later Webster in his forcible rhetoric declared :
"The truth is, sir, that party support is not the kind of support necessary to sustain the country through a long, expen-
sive, and bloody contest ; and this should have been considered
before the war was declared. The cause, to be successful, must
be upheld by other sentiments and higher motives. It must
draw to itself the sober approbation of the great mass of the
people. It must enlist, not their temporary or party feelings,
but their steady patriotism and their constant zeal. Unlike
the old nations of Europe, there are in this country no dregs
of population fit only to supply the constant waste of war and
out of which an army can be raised for hire at any time and
for any purpose. Armies of any magnitude can be here nothing but the people embodied ; and if the object be one for which
the people will not embody there can be no armies."[3]

[1] Noted by Von Holst, I. 256.
[2] Benton, Ab. Debates of Congress, IV. 452.
[3] Benton, Ab. Debates of Congress, V. 139.

But previously, in his celebrated Fourth of July oration at Portsmouth, in 1812,[1] Webster had taken the ground that the war was unjustifiable in political economy, but that it was now legally declared and had become the law of the land, and all citizens, including those of New England, although they saw that their personal interests had been disregarded, should pay their share of the expenses and render personal service to the full and just extent of their constitutional liability. Here the old question again arose. Who is to decide what that constitutional liability includes? And here again is seen the absurd and disgraceful position of the once-honored Federalists. All of the New England legislatures, excepting that of Vermont, as well as that of New Jersey, planted themselves upon the ground marked out for them by Webster, with the further and, in the light of the past history of the men engaged in the movement, ludicrously extreme position taken by the Supreme Court of Massachusetts and the military commander of Rhode Island. The outgrowth of this doctrine was the refusal of militia aid by New England and, a little later, the Hartford Convention.[2]

Upon the history and work of the Hartford Convention we need not dwell longer than to recall the fact that the states in sending delegates to the Convention were committing an extra-constitutional and, to say the least, highly unnational act, that their report read like a revised edition of Madison's Virginia Resolutions, that they urged specific constitutional amendments, some of which—notably those calling for the prohibition of commercial intercourse, the admission of new states, and the declaration of war by a two-thirds majority only of both houses of Congress—sound strangely like process under the old Confederation régime, 1781-7. As showing the anti-

---

[1] Curtis, Life of Daniel Webster, I. 105. Cf. Webster's Speech in the House of Representatives, January 14th, 1814, Benton, Ab. Debates of Congress, V. 138.
[2] Von Holst, 1. 260-272; Hildreth, VI. 472, 473, 532 535, 545-558. Cf. Dwight, History of the Hartford Convention.

national tendencies prevalent at the time, the report of the Hartford Convention is of interest to us. But the almost immediate conclusion of peace put an end to any attempts to carry out its suggestions.

With the conclusion of the war came a calm, and in its quiet we are able to discern what were the effects of the conflict upon the great internal question in the United States.

Looking back from our standpoint of the present we can easily conclude that as a matter of right the war was certainly fully justified, but as an economic policy its expediency must be questioned. It had lasted two and one-half years and raised the national debt from $45,000,000 to $127,000,000, or at the rate of somewhat more than $30,000,000 a year. Yet its political effect was cheaply bought even at that price. Although not destined to be permanent, the national feeling it produced was something entirely novel, but none the less excellent.

From 1800 to 1815 the old national party, the Federalists, driven by the necessities of opposition and selfishness, gravitated over to the particularistic doctrine, but lost weight at each step, until finally, like a candle burned to its socket, they flickered faintly in the Hartford Convention and then went out forever. On the other hand, the Republicans, led by the possession of power and, it were charitable to suppose, a more enlightened intelligence, grew stronger day by day as they gave up, in practice at least, their old particularistic and strict construction theories for a more broadly national platform. That the sentiment of the people at large had correspondingly changed is shown by the next presidential election. When the votes of the election for the eighth presidential term were counted, it was found that only 34 out of 217 had been cast for Federalist candidates. Even Rhode Island now severed her connection with her old friends, Massachusetts and Connecticut, although Delaware now joined them. How demoralized the Federalist party had become appears still more clearly when we see how their votes for Vice-President were scattered.

Massachusetts voted solidly for John Eager Howard of Maryland, Delaware did the same for Robert G. Harper of Maryland, while Connecticut gave five votes to James Ross of Pennsylvania and four to John Marshall of Virginia. These three states alone cast any electoral votes against the Republican candidates. The Republicans now, for the instant at any rate, a national party, remained masters of the field and until circumstances should develop new party issues their supremacy was assured.

Strangely enough sound the testimonies to the unifying influence of the war given by men who belonged to the same party that Jefferson had once led. And we know of no better way to show this effect of the war than by a few selections from the political correspondence of the leading men of the period.

Almost with a voice of prophecy Gallatin had written to Nicholson, July 17th, 1807, in regard to the war which was even then looked forward to : " In fact the greatest mischiefs which I apprehend from the war are the necessary increase of executive power and influence . . . and the introduction of permanent military and naval establishments,"[1] both of which we know to be the concomitants of a perfect nation.

September 6th, 1815, Gallatin writes to Jefferson, then in retirement at Monticello : " The war has been useful. The character of America stands now as high as ever on the European continent and higher than it ever did in Great Britain. I may say that we are favorites everywhere except at courts, and even there we are personally respected and considered as the nation designed to check the naval despotism of England."[2]

Again he writes to Jefferson, under the date of November 27th, 1815 : " The war has been successfully and honorably terminated ; a debt of no more than eighty millions incurred, Louisiana paid for, and an incipient navy created ; our popu-

---

[1] Henry Adams, The Writings of Albert Gallatin, I. 339.
[2] Adams, Writings of Albert Gallatin, I. 651, 652.

lation increased in the same and our resources in a much greater proportion; our revenue greater than ever." [1]

Gallatin says to Matthew Lyon,[2] May 7th, 1816: "The war has been productive of evil and good, but I think the good preponderates. Independent of the loss of lives and of the losses in property by individuals, the war has laid the foundation of permanent taxes and military establishments which the Republicans had deemed unfavorable to the happiness and free institutions of the country. But under our former system we were becoming too selfish, too much attached exclusively to the acquisition of wealth, above all, too much confined in our political feelings to local and State objects. The war has renewed and reinstated the national feelings and character which the Revolution had given and which were daily lessened. The people have now more general objects of attachment with which their pride and political opinions are connected. They are more Americans; they feel and act more as a nation, and I hope that the permanency of the Union is thereby better secured." [3]

And twenty years later, when the smoke of the old battle had cleared away and another conflict, this time one of principles, was waging, Gallatin writes to Edward Everett, January, 1835: "I do insist on the undeniable fact that the national character has been entirely redeemed by the late war, and that at this time no country is held by foreign nations and governments in higher respect and consideration than the United States." [4]

---

[1] Adams, Writings of Albert Gallatin, I. 667.

[2] Matthew Lyon represented a Vermont district in the House of Representatives from 1797 to 1801, and a Kentucky district from 1803 to 1811. For some of the incidents of his sensational political career, see Hildreth, V. 80, 187-191, 247-250, 295; VI. 238, 239; and also McMaster, A History of the People of the United States from the Revolution to the Civil War. New York, D. Appleton & Company, 1885. Vol. II. pp. 327-329, 356, 363-367, 399-402, 430, 532.

[3] Adams, Writings of Albert Gallatin, I. 700.

[4] Adams, Writings of Albert Gallatin, II. 500.

Jefferson writes to Gallatin, May 18th, 1816, in reference to the lack of political dissension in Virginia, and says: "This spontaneous and universal concurrence of sentiment has not been artificially produced. I consider this as presenting an element of character in our people which must constitute the basis of every estimate of the solidity and duration of our government."[1] Strange words these to come from the pen which drew up the Kentucky resolutions!

Crawford, in a letter to Gallatin, bearing the date of October 27th, 1817, writes: "The President's tour through the East has produced something like a political jubilee. They were in the land of steady habits, at least for the time, 'all Federalists, all Republicans.' A general absolution of political sins seems to have been mutually agreed upon."[2]

The war had ruined the particularists; it had made all nationalists, if we may use the word. The bonds of the early days of the revolution were forged anew and the nation's heart beat as one. Patriotism and national pride had conquered sectionalism and personal selfishness. The era of good feeling had dawned.[3] But it was the ominous calm that precedes the tempest.

With this position gained and all foreign entanglements removed by Waterloo and its consequences, the United States was thrown back on itself and the fire of slavery which had been smoldering in its bosom now found an opportunity to burst forth afresh and kindle the conflagration from which

---

[1] Adams, Writings of Albert Gallatin, I. 705.
[2] Adams, Writings of Albert Gallatin, II. 55; Hildreth, VI. 623.
[3] Owing to the fact that this essay was written before the excellent History of the United States of America under the Constitution, by James Schouler, Washington, 1886, was published, no references to that work are made. Volumes I. and II. of Mr. Schouler's History, embracing the period discussed in this monograph, are particularly important for the proper understanding of the influences at work in it. In Vol. II. 452–454, it is gratifying to find the author taking the view of the effect of the War of 1812 that is developed in this essay.

the camp-fires of the great civil war forty years later were to be lighted.

But because the good effect of the second war with Great Britain was soon swept away by the slavery dispute, we must not overlook the fact that such an effect existed. The country entered the war distracted, indifferent, and particularistic; it emerged from it united, enthusiastic, and national. But the ebb was to be greater than the flow, and half a century was to elapse before the conditions of national unity which existed in the years immediately following the war of 1812 were again to be plainly observed in our political history.

PUBLICATIONS OF THE

JOHNS HOPKINS UNIVERSITY
BALTIMORE

I. **American Journal of Mathematics.**
S. NEWCOMB, Editor, and T. CRAIG, Associate Editor. Quarterly. 4to.
Volume IX in progress. $5 per volume.

II. **American Chemical Journal.**
I. REMSEN, Editor. Bi-monthly. 8vo. Volume IX in progress. $3 per
volume.

III. **American Journal of Philology.**
B. L. GILDERSLEEVE, Editor. Quarterly. 8vo. Volume VIII in progress.
$3 per volume.

IV. **Studies from the Biological Laboratory.**
Including the Chesapeake Zoölogical Laboratory. II. N. MARTIN, Editor,
and W. K. BROOKS, Associate Editor. 8vo. Volume IV in progress.
$5 per volume.

V. **Studies in Historical and Political Science.**
II. B. ADAMS, Editor. Monthly. 8vo. Volume V in progress. $3 per
volume.

VI. **Johns Hopkins University Circulars.**
Containing reports of scientific and literary work in progress in Baltimore.
4to. Vol. VI in progress. $1 per year.

VII. **Annual Report.**
Presented by the President to the Board of Trustees, reviewing the operations of the University during the past academic year.

VIII. **Annual Register.**
Giving the list of officers and students, and stating the regulations, etc., of the
University. *Published at the close of the academic year.*

ROWLAND'S PHOTOGRAPH OF THE NORMAL SOLAR SPECTRUM. Set of seven
plates unmounted $10, mounted $12; single plates unmounted $2, mounted
$2.25. 1886.

REPRODUCTION IN PHOTOTYPE OF A SYRIAC MS. WITH THE ANTILEGOMENA
EPISTLES. Edited by I. H. Hall. 1886. $3, paper; $4, cloth.

STUDIES IN LOGIC. By members of the Johns Hopkins University. C. S. Peirce,
Editor. (Boston. Little, Brown & Co.) 1883. 123 pp. 12mo. $2.00.

THE DEVELOPMENT AND PROPAGATION OF THE OYSTER IN MARYLAND. By
W. K. Brooks. 1884. 193 pp. 4to; 13 plates and 3 maps. $5.00.

ON THE MECHANICAL EQUIVALENT OF HEAT. By H. A. Rowland. 1880.
127 pp. 8vo. $1.50.

NEW TESTAMENT AUTOGRAPHS. By J. Rendel Harris. 1882. 54 pp. 8vo; 4
plates. 50 cents.

SELECTED MORPHOLOGICAL MONOGRAPHS. W. K. Brooks, Editor. Vol. I.
1887. 370 pp. and 51 plates. 4to. $7.50, cloth.

Communications in respect to exchanges and remittances may be
sent to the Johns Hopkins University (Publication Agency), Baltimore, Maryland.

LAW BOOKS,
PUBLISHED BY
CUSHINGS & BAILEY,
BALTIMORE, MD.

ALEXANDER'S BRITISH STATUTES IN FORCE IN MARY-LAND. 1 vol. 8vo...	$10 00
BARROLL'S MARYLAND CHANCERY PRACTICE. 1 vol. 8vo...	3 00
BLAND'S " " REPORTS. 3 vols. 8vo....	15 00
BUMP'S FEDERAL PROCEDURE. 1 vol. 8vo..............................	6 50
" FRAUDULENT CONVEYANCES. Third Edition. 1 vol. 8vo...	6 50
EVANS' MARYLAND COMMON LAW PRACTICE. 1 vol. 8vo.....	4 00
HINKLEY & MAYER ON LAW OF ATTACHMENT IN MARY-LAND. 1 vol. 8vo...	3 00
MARYLAND DIGEST, BY NORRIS, BROWN & BRUNE. Comprising Harris & McHenry, 4 vols.;—Harris & Johnson, 7 vols.;—Harris & Gill, 2 vols.;—Gill & Johnson, 12 vols.;—Bland's Chancery, 3 vols..........	10 00
" DIGEST, BY STOCKETT, MERRICK & MILLER. Comprising Gill, 9 vols.;—Maryland, 1-8 inc.;—Johnson's Chancery, 4 vols.............................	10 00
" DIGEST, BY COHEN & LEE. Comprising 9-20 inc. Maryland.........................	10 00
" DIGEST, BY BURGWYN. Comprising 21 to 45 inc. Maryland......................	10 00
POE'S PLEADING AND PRACTICE. 2 vols. Vol. 1, Pleading. Second Edition in press. " 2, Practice...	7 00
GROUND RENTS IN MARYLAND. By LEWIS MAYER, ESQ., of the Baltimore Bar. 1 vol...	1 50
MARYLAND REPORTS. 60 vols. 1851 to 1883. Per vol...............	4 00

A few *complete* sets of Maryland Reports on hand at present, comprising: Harris & McHenry's Reports, 4 vols.;—Harris & Johnson's Reports, 7 vols.;—Harris & Gill's Reports, 2 vols.;—Gill & Johnson's Reports, 12 vols.;—Gill's Reports, 9 vols.;—Maryland Reports, 60 vols.;—Bland's Chancery Reports, 3 vols.;—Johnson's Chancery Reports, 4 vols.;—101 vols. For sale cheap.

They also keep a large and complete stock of Law, Classical, Medical and Miscellaneous Publications, which they offer for sale at low prices.

Agents for Sale of the Publications of the Johns Hopkins University.

THE MAGAZINE OF AMERICAN HISTORY.

THE MAGAZINE OF AMERICAN HISTORY,

An illustrated monthly devoted to history, and the literature, antiquities, and curiosities of history, which, being popular and pleasing in style, has achieved unparalleled success. It deals with every problem in American history, from the most remote period to the present hour, and it is as readable as any work of fiction. Its SEVENTEENTH VOLUME begins with the January number, 1887.

SUBSCRIPTION PRICE, $5 A YEAR IN ADVANCE.

To public libraries and reading rooms, and to all educational institutions this magazine has long since become an actual necessity.

It is also one of the best of household journals, and it has the largest circulation of any magazine of its character in the world.

Having grown remarkably prosperous during the past year, it is now prepared to extend its usefulness to every quarter of the country, and to foreign lands. It will continue to offer

COMBINATION SUBSCRIPTION RATES,

as this method has proved a great convenience to persons residing at a distance, and particularly to schools, colleges, and reading rooms.

Magazine of American History, and the Forum,	$ 8 00
Magazine of American History, The Century, and Harper's Magazine,	10 50
Magazine of American History, and Good Housekeeping,	6 00
Magazine of American History, and The North American Review,	8 00
Magazine of American History, and The Andover Review,	7 00
Magazine of American History, The Nation, and Army and Navy Journal,	12 00
Magazine of American History, The Critic, and New York Observer,	10 00
Magazine of American History, St. Nicholas, and Scientific American,	10 00
Magazine of American History, Babyhood, and New York Independent,	8 50
Magazine of American History, and The Southern Bivouac,	6 00
Magazine of American History, and Queries,	5 25

Any other desired combination of leading periodicals will be furnished; price quoted on application.

There are two handsome volumes in each year, beginning with January and July.

The price of the bound volume is $3.50 for each half year, in dark green levant cloth, and $4.50 if bound in half morocco. Address

MAGAZINE OF AMERICAN HISTORY,
30 Lafayette Place, New York City.

THE AMERICAN JOURNAL OF ARCHÆOLOGY

AND OF THE

HISTORY OF THE FINE ARTS.

The Journal is the organ of the Archæological Institute of America, and covers all branches of Archæology and Art History: Oriental, Classical, Early Christian, Mediaeval and American. It is intended to supply a record of the important work done in the field of Archæology, under the following categories: I. Original Articles; II. Correspondence; III. Reviews of Books; IV. Archæological News, presenting a careful and ample record of discoveries and investigations in all parts of the world; V. Summaries of the principal archæological periodicals.

No. 4 for 1886 is ready and contains articles

(1) By Prof. John H. Wright, on *Some inedited Greek Lekythoi* in American collections:

(2) By Dr. Alfred Emerson, on the *Portraiture of Alexander the Great and a Terracotta Head in Munich:*

(3) By Prof. A. L. Frothingham, Jr., on *The Mosaics of the Portico of St. John Lateran at Rome.*

Profs. F. X. Kraus and Merriam contribute notes and X, a distinguished French archæologist, writes on the recent meetings of societies in France. Mr. Russell Sturgis, Hon. John Worthington and Prof. Frothingham contribute book reviews, and the usual *News* and *Summaries* complete the number.

The Journal is published quarterly, and forms a yearly volume of about 450 pages royal 8vo, with plates and figures, at the subscription price of $3.50. Vol. I (1885), bound in cloth, containing over 480 pages, 11 plates and 16 figures, will be sent post-paid on receipt of $4.

A. L. FROTHINGHAM, Jr., Managing Editor,
29 Cathedral Street, Baltimore, Md.

HISTORY.

Students and Teachers of History will find the following to be invaluable aids:—

STUDIES IN GENERAL HISTORY.

(1000 B. C. to 1880 A. D.) An application of the Scientific Method to the Teaching of History. By MARY D. SHELDON, formerly Prof. of History in Wellesley College. Price by mail, $1.75.

This book has been prepared in order that the general student may share in the advantages of the Seminary Method of Instruction. It is a collection of historic material, interspersed with problems whose answers the student must work out for himself from original historical data. In this way he is trained to deal with the original historical data of his own time. In short, it may be termed *an exercise book in history and politics.*

THE TEACHER'S MANUAL contains the continuous statement of the results which should be gained from the History, and embodies the teacher's part of the work, being made up of summaries, explanations, and suggestions for essays and examinations. Price by mail, 85 cts.

SHELDON'S STUDIES IN GREEK AND ROMAN HISTORY.

Price by mail, $1.10. Meets the needs of students preparing for college, of schools in which Ancient History takes the place of General History, and of students who have used an ordinary manual, and wish to make a spirited and helpful review.

METHODS OF TEACHING AND STUDYING HISTORY.

Edited by G. STANLEY HALL, Professor of Psychology and Pedagogy in Johns Hopkins University. Price by mail, $1.40.

Contains, in the form most likely to be of direct practical utility to teachers, as well as to students and readers of history, the opinions and modes of instruction, actual or ideal, of eminent and representative specialists in leading American and English universities.

SELECT BIBLIOGRAPHY OF CHURCH HISTORY.

By J. A. FISHER, Johns Hopkins University. Price by mail, 20 cents.

HISTORY TOPICS FOR HIGH SCHOOLS AND COLLEGES.

With an Introduction upon the Topical Method of Instruction in History. By WM. FRANCIS ALLEN, Professor in the University of Wisconsin. Price by mail, 30 cents.

LARGE OUTLINE MAP OF THE UNITED STATES.

Edited by EDWARD CHANNING, Ph.D., and ALBERT B. HART, Ph.D., Instructors in History in Harvard University. For the use of Classes in History, in Geography, and in Geology. Price by mail 60 cents.

SMALL OUTLINE MAP OF THE UNITED STATES.

For the Desk of the Pupil. Prepared by EDWARD CHANNING, Ph.D, and ALBERT B. HART, Ph.D., Instructors in Harvard University. Price, 2 cents each, or $1.50 per hundred.

We publish also small Outline Maps of North America, South America, Europe, Central and Western Europe, Asia, Africa, Great Britain and the World on Mercator's Projection. These maps will be found invaluable to classes in history, for use in locating prominent historical points, and for indicating physical features, political boundaries, and the progress of historical growth. Price, 2 cents each, or $1.50 per hundred.

POLITICAL AND PHYSICAL WALL MAPS.

We handle both the JOHNSTON and STANFORD series, and can always supply teachers and schools at the lowest rates. Correspondence solicited.

D. C. HEATH & CO., Publishers, Boston, New York and Chicago.

THE PHILOSOPHY OF WEALTH.

ECONOMIC PRINCIPLES NEWLY FORMULATED. By JOHN B. CLARK, A. M., Professor of History and Political Science in Smith College; Lecturer on Political Economy in Amherst College. Mailing price, $1.10; for Introduction, $1.00.

In general, this work is **a restatement of economic principles in harmony with the modern spirit,** discarding the Ricardian method, free from *doctrinaireism* and pessimism, and recognizing the operation of higher motives of action than pure self-interest.

In particular, the work aims to secure a more philosophical conception of wealth, labor, and value, and of the economic processes considered as activities of the social organism; it attempts to lay a foundation for the solution of the labor problem, by presenting a Theory of Distribution in which account is taken of the growing solidarity of capital and of labor, of the narrowing limits of competition, and of the increasing field afforded for the action of moral forces.

The book is intended for general readers, and, while not in the form of a text-book, and not a complete discussion of political economy, may be used with advantage by classes whose teachers instruct partly by lectures and topical reading.

The clearness and originality of the thought, and the freshness of the style, serve to render the work singularly stimulating and suggestive as well as instructive.

THE POLITICAL SCIENCE QUARTERLY, edited by the Faculty of Political Science of Columbia College. Annual subscription, $3.00.

"A Review of great promise."—*Journal des Économistes,* Paris.

MACY'S OUR GOVERNMENT. Mailing price, 88 cents.

GINN & COMPANY, Publishers,
Boston, New York, and Chicago.

American Economic Association,

Organized at Saratoga, September 9, 1885.

President.
FRANCIS A. WALKER, LL. D., . . . Massachusetts Institute of Technology.

Vice-Presidents.
HENRY C. ADAMS, Ph. D., . University of Michigan and Cornell University.
EDMUND J. JAMES, Ph. D., ... University of Pennsylvania.
JOHN B. CLARK, A. M., ... Smith College.

Secretary.
RICHARD T. ELY, Ph. D.,
Address: Johns Hopkins University, Baltimore, Md.

Treasurer.
EDWIN R. A. SELIGMAN, Ph. D., ... Columbia College.
Address: 26 West 34th Street, New York.

OBJECTS.
1. The encouragement of economic research.
2. The publication of economic monographs.
3. The encouragement of perfect freedom in all economic discussion.
4. The establishment of a Bureau of Information designed to aid members in their economic studies.

PUBLICATIONS.

No. 1. **Report of the Organization of the American Economic Association.** By RICHARD T. ELY, Ph. D., Secretary. Price 50 cents.

Nos. 2 and 3. **The Relation of the Modern Municipality to the Gas Supply.** By EDMUND J. JAMES, Ph. D., of the Wharton School of Finance and Economy, University of Pennsylvania. Price 75 cents.

No. 4. **Coöperation in a Western City.** By ALBERT SHAW, Ph. D., Editor of the *Minneapolis Tribune,* Author of *Icaria,* etc. Price 75 cents.

No. 5. **Coöperation in New England.** By EDWARD W. BEMIS, Ph. D. Price 75 cents.

No. 6. **Relation of the State to Industrial Action.** By HENRY C. ADAMS, Ph. D., of the University of Michigan and Cornell University. Price 75 cents.

VOL. II.

No. 1. **Three Phases of Coöperation in the West.** By AMOS G. WARNER, Fellow of the Johns Hopkins University. Price 75 cents.

No. 2. **Historical Sketch of the Finances of Pennsylvania.** By T. K. WORTHINGTON, A. B. With an Introduction by RICHARD T. ELY, Ph. D. Price 75 cents.

The publications of the Association will number at least six a year, and will be sent to all members in consideration of the annual membership fee of $3 paid to the Treasurer. To others the publications of the Association will be sent at $4 per annum.

Communications may be addressed to the Secretary,

RICHARD T. ELY,
Johns Hopkins University, Baltimore, Md.

The Republic of New Haven.

A History of Municipal Evolution.

By CHARLES H. LEVERMORE, Ph. D.

Fellow in History, 1884-85, Johns Hopkins University.

(Extra Volume One of Studies in Historical and Political Science.)

This work is a new study, from original records, of a most remarkable chapter of municipal development. Beginning with an English germ in the Parish of St. Stephen, Coleman Street, London, Dr. Levermore has traced the evolution of the Rev. John Davenport's church into a veritable commonwealth, in which the life-forces of Old England circulate anew.

The Republic of New Haven is unique and one of the most interesting of all American commonwealths. It was a city-state, self-contained, self-sufficing, like the municipal commonwealths of antiquity. It is impossible to measure the greatness of Greek cities or of the Italian republics by their extent of territory. It is equally impossible to estimate the colonial and municipal life of America by any standards of material greatness. And yet few persons realize how far-reaching in American History is the influence of a single town like New Haven. Not to speak of the intellectual forces which have gone forth from that local republic, from its vigorous church-life and from Yale College, born of the Church, New Haven, like her Mother England, is the parent of a wide-spread colonial system, not unworthy of comparison with that of Greek cities.

The volume comprises 342 pages octavo, with various diagrams and an index. It will be sold, neatly bound in cloth, at $2.00. Subscribers to the STUDIES can obtain at reduced rates this volume, bound uniformly with the First, Second, Third, and Fourth Series.

Orders should be addressed to THE PUBLICATION AGENCY OF THE JOHNS HOPKINS UNIVERSITY, BALTIMORE, MARYLAND.

PHILADELPHIA

1681-1887:

A History of Municipal Development.

By Edward P. Allinson, A. M., and Boies Penrose, A. B.,

OF THE PHILADELPHIA BAR.

(*Extra Volume Two of Studies in Historical and Political Science.*)

While several general histories of Philadelphia have been written, there is no history of that city as a municipal corporation. Such a work is now offered, based upon the Acts of Assembly, the City Ordinances, the State Reports, and many other authorities. Numerous manuscripts in the Pennsylvania Historical Society, in Public Libraries, and in the Departments at Philadelphia and Harrisburg have also been consulted, and important facts found therein are now for the first time published.

The history of the government of the city begins with the mediæval charter of most contracted character, and ends with *the liberal provisions of the Reform Act of 1885*. It furnishes illustrations of almost every phase of municipal development. The story cannot fail to interest all those who believe that the question of better government for our great cities is one of critical importance, and who are aware of the fact that this question is already receiving widespread attention. The subject had become so serious in 1876 that Governor Hartranft, in his message of that year, called the attention of the Legislature to it in the following succinct and forcible statement: " *There is no political problem that at the present moment occasions so much just alarm and is obtaining more anxious thought than the government of cities.*"

The volume comprises 444 pages, octavo, and will be sold, bound in cloth, at $3; in law-sheep at $3.50; and at reduced rates to regular subscribers to the " Studies."

Orders should be addressed to The Publication Agency of the Johns Hopkins University, Baltimore, Maryland.

BALTIMORE

NINETEENTH OF APRIL, 1861.

A Study of the War.

By GEORGE WILLIAM BROWN,

Chief Judge of the Supreme Bench of Baltimore and Mayor of the City in 1861.

(Extra Volume Three of Studies in Historical and Political Science.)

The position of Judge Brown as Mayor of Baltimore in 1861 gave him exceptional opportunities for observing and understanding the municipal situation. His unflinching devotion to official duty in marching through Pratt Street at the head of the Massachusetts Sixth Regiment, on the 19th of April, in the midst of a furious mob, will inspire confidence in his account of the events of that day. The concurrent testimony of Baltimoreans, of different political opinions, confirms Judge Brown's historical statement as the most accurate that has thus far been written. The events leading to the 19th of April and immediately following that date are frankly discussed. Judge Brown's point of view is that of many leading citizens of Maryland. He has attempted to describe the position of the middle, or peace party. Judge Brown's Study is a contribution to a better understanding of the state of society and of public feeling in the border land between the North and the South in 1861. After the lapse of a quarter of a century, American citizens have learned to hear with interest and appreciation both sides in the story of battles and campaigns. A Maryland view of past Politics may serve to enlighten the Present and instruct the Future.

The volume comprises 176 pages, octavo, and will be sold, bound in cloth, at $1; and at reduced rates to regular subscribers to the "Studies."

Orders should be addressed to THE PUBLICATION AGENCY OF THE JOHNS HOPKINS UNIVERSITY, BALTIMORE, MARYLAND.

MODERN LANGUAGE NOTES.

A MONTHLY PUBLICATION

(For eight months in the year)

DEVOTED TO THE INTERESTS

OF THE

ACADEMIC STUDY OF ENGLISH, GERMAN,

AND THE

ROMANCE LANGUAGES.

A. MARSHALL ELLIOTT, *Managing Editor.*

JAMES W. BRIGHT, JULIUS GOEBEL, HENRY ALFRED TODD, *Associate Editors.*

This is a new and successfully-launched periodical, managed by a corps of professors and instructors in the Johns Hopkins University, with the co-operation of many of the leading college professors, in the department of modern languages, throughout the country. While undertaking to maintain a high critical and scientific standard, the new journal will endeavor to engage the interest and meet the wants of the entire class of serious and progressive modern-language teachers, of whatever grade. Since its establishment in January, 1886, the journal has been repeatedly enlarged, and has met with constantly increasing encouragement and success. The wide range of its articles, original, critical, literary and pedagogical, by a number of the foremost American (and European) scholars, has well represented and recorded the recent progress of modern language studies, both at home and abroad.

The list of contributors to MODERN LANGUAGE NOTES, in addition to the Editors, includes, to the present time, the following names:—

ANDERSON, MELVILLE B, De Pauw University, Ind.; BANCROFT, T. WHITING, Brown University, R. I.; BASKERVILL, W. M., Vanderbilt University, Tenn.; BOCHER, FERDINAND, Harvard University, Mass.; BRADLEY, C. B., University of California. Cal.; BRANDT, H. C. G., Hamilton College, N. Y.; BROWNE, WM. HAND, Johns Hopkins University, Md.; BURNHAM, WM. H., Johns Hopkins University, Md.; CARPENTER, WM H., Columbia College, N. Y.; CLÉDAT, L., Faculté des Lettres, Lyons, France; COHN, ADOLPHE, Harvard University, Mass.; COOK, A. S., University of California, Cal.; COSIJN, P. J., University of Leyden, Holland; CRANE, T. F., Cornell University, N. Y.; DAVIDSON, THOMAS, Orange, N. J.; EGGE, ALBERT E., Johns Hopkins University, Md.; FAY, E. A., National Deaf-Mute College, Washington, D. C.; FORTIER, ALCÉE, Tulane University, La.; GARNER, SAMUEL, Indiana University, Ind.; GERBER, A., Earlham College, Ind.; GRANDGENT, CHARLES, Harvard University, Mass.; GUMMERE, F. B., The Swain Free School, Mass.; HART, J. M., University of Cincinnati, Ohio; HEMPL, GEO., University of Göttingen, Germany; HUSS, H. C. O., Princeton College, N. J.; VON JAGEMANN, H. C. G., University of Indiana, Ind.; KARSTEN, GUSTAF, University of Geneva, Switzerland; LANG, HENRY R., The Swain Free School, Mass.; LEARNED, M. D., Johns Hopkins University, Md.; LEYH, EDW. F., Baltimore, Md; LODEMAN, A., State Normal School, Mich.; MORFILL, W. R., Oxford, England; McCABE, T., Johns Hopkins University, Md.; McELROY, JOHN G. R., University of Pennsylvania, Pa.; O'CONNOR, B. F., Columbia College, N. Y.; PRIMER, SYLVESTER, College of Charleston, S. C.; SCHELE DE VERE, M., University of Virginia, Va.; SCHILLING, HUGO, Wittenberg College, Ohio; SHELDON, EDW. S., Harvard University, Mass.; SHEPHERD, H. E., College of Charleston, S. C.; SCHMIDT, H., University of North Carolina, N. C.; SIEVERS, EDUARD, University of Tübingen, Germany; SMYTH, A. H., High School of Philadelphia, Pa.; STODDARD, FRANCIS H., University of California, Cal.; STÜRZINGER, J. J., Bryn Mawr College, Pa.; THOMAS, CALVIN, University of Michigan, Mich.; WALTER, E. L., University of Michigan, Mich.; WARREN, F. M., Johns Hopkins University, Md.; WHITE, H. S., Cornell University, N. Y.; ZDANOWICZ, CASIMIR, Vanderbilt University, Tenn.

SUBSCRIPTION PRICE ONE DOLLAR PER ANNUM IN THE U. S.
$1.25 FOR FOREIGN COUNTRIES IN THE POSTAL UNION.
SINGLE COPIES FIFTEEN CENTS.

Specimen pages sent on application.

Subscriptions, advertisements and all business communications should be addressed to the

MANAGING EDITOR OF MODERN LANGUAGE NOTES,

JOHNS HOPKINS UNIVERSITY, BALTIMORE, MD.

JOHNS HOPKINS UNIVERSITY STUDIES

IN

HISTORICAL AND POLITICAL SCIENCE

HERBERT B. ADAMS, Editor

History is past Politics and Politics present History — *Freeman*

FIFTH SERIES

VII

The Effect of the War of 1812

UPON THE

CONSOLIDATION OF THE UNION

By NICHOLAS MURRAY BUTLER, Ph. D.

Tutor in Philosophy in Columbia College
President of the Industrial Education Association's College for the Training of Teachers

BALTIMORE

PUBLICATION AGENCY OF THE JOHNS HOPKINS UNIVERSITY

JULY, 1887

PRICE TWENTY-FIVE CENTS

JOHNS HOPKINS UNIVERSITY STUDIES
IN
Historical and Political Science.

HERBERT B. ADAMS, Editor.

Neither the University nor the Editor assumes responsibility for the views of contributors.

PROSPECTUS OF FIFTH SERIES.—1887.

The Studies in Municipal Government will be continued. The following papers are ready or in preparation:—

I-II.　City Government of Philadelphia. By EDWARD P. ALLINSON, A. M. (Haverford) and BOIES PENROSE, A. B. (Harvard). January and February, 1887. *Price 50 cents.* 72 pp.

III.　City Government of Boston. By JAMES M. BUGBEE. March, 1887. *Price 25 cents.* 60 pp.

IV.　City Government of St. Louis. By MARSHALL S. SNOW, A. M. (Harvard), Professor of History, Washington University. April, 1887. *Price 25 cents.* 40 pp.

V-VI.　Local Government in Canada. By JOHN GEORGE BOURINOT, LL. D. Clerk of the House of Commons of Canada. May and June, 1887. *Price 50 cents.* 72 pp.

VII.　The Influence of the War of 1812 upon the Consolidation of the American Union. By NICHOLAS MURRAY BUTLER, Ph. D. and Fellow of Columbia College. July, 1887. *Price 25 cents.* 30 pp.

City Government of Baltimore. By JOHN C. ROSE, B. L. (University of Maryland, School of Law).

City Government of Chicago. By F. H. HODDER, Ph. M. (University of Mich.); Instructor in History, Cornell University.

City Government of San Francisco. By BERNARD MOSES, Ph. D.; Professor of History and Politics, University of California.

City Government of New Orleans. By HON. W. W. HOWE.

City Government of New York. By SIMON STERNE and J. F. JAMESON Ph. D., Associate in History, J. H. U.

The History of American Political Economy. Studies by R. T. ELY, WOODROW WILSON, and D. R. DEWEY.

FOURTH SERIES.—Municipal Government and Land Tenure.—1886.

I.　Dutch Village Communities on the Hudson River. By IRVING ELTING, A. B. (Harvard). *Price 50 cents.*

II-III.　Town Government in Rhode Island. By W. E. FOSTER, A. M. (Brown).—The Narragansett Planters. By EDWARD CHANNING, Ph. D. (Harvard). *Price 50 cents.*

IV.　Pennsylvania Boroughs. By WILLIAM P. HOLCOMB, Ph. D. (J. H. U.), Professor of History, Swarthmore College. *Price 50 cents.*

V.　Introduction to the Constitutional and Political History of the individual States. By J. F. JAMESON, Ph. D. and Associate in History, J. H. U. *Price 50 cents.*

VI.　The Puritan Colony at Annapolis, Maryland. By DANIEL R. RANDALL, Fellow in History (J. H. U.). *Price 50 cents.*

VII-VIII-IX.　History of the Land Question in the United States. By SHOSUKE SATO, Ph. D. and Fellow by Courtesy, J. H. U. *Price $1.00.*

X.　The Town and City Government of New Haven. [Chapters VIII and IX from Levermore's "Republic of New Haven."] By CHARLES H. LEVERMORE, Ph. D. (J. H. U.), Instructor in History, University of California. *Price 50 cents.*

XI-XII.　The Land System of the New England Colonies. By MELVILLE EGLESTON, A. M. (Williams College). *Price 50 cents.*

(*Continued on third page of cover.*)

THIRD SERIES.—Maryland, Virginia and Washington.—1885.

I. **Maryland's Influence upon Land Cessions to the United States.** With minor papers on George Washington's Interest in Western Lands, the Potomac Company, and a National University. By H. B. ADAMS. *Price 75 cents.*

II-III. **Virginia Local Institutions:—The Land System; Hundred; Parish; County; Town.** By EDWARD INGLE, A. B. (J. H. U.) *Price 75 cents.*

IV. **Recent American Socialism.** By RICHARD T. ELY. *Price 50 cents.*

V-VI-VII. **Maryland Local Institutions:—The Land System; Hundred; County; Town.** By LEWIS W. WILHELM, Ph. D. and Fellow by Courtesy, J. H. U. *Price $1.00.*

VIII. **The Influence of the Proprietors in Founding the State of New Jersey.** By Professor AUSTIN SCOTT (Rutgers College). *Price 25 cents.*

IX-X. **American Constitutions; The Relations of the Three Departments as Adjusted by a Century.** By HORACE DAVIS. *Price 50 cents.*

XI-XII. **The City of Washington.** By J. A. PORTER, A. B. (Yale). *Price 50 cents.*

SECOND SERIES.—Institutions and Economics.—1884.

I-II. **Methods of Historical Study.** By H. B. ADAMS. *Price 50 cents.*

III. **The Past and the Present of Political Economy.** By R. T. ELY. *Price 35 cents.*

IV. **Samuel Adams, The Man of the Town Meeting.** By Professor JAMES K. HOSMER (Washington University, St. Louis). *Price 35 cents.*

V-VI. **Taxation in the United States.** By HENRY CARTER ADAMS, Ph. D. (J. H. U.); University of Michigan. *Price 50 cents.*

VII. **Institutional Beginnings in a Western State.** By Professor JESSE MACY (Iowa College). *Price 25 cents.*

VIII-IX. **Indian Money as a Factor in New England Civilization.** By WILLIAM B. WEEDEN, A. M. (Brown Univ.) *Price 50 cents.*

X. **Town and County Government in the English Colonies of North America.** By EDWARD CHANNING, Ph. D. (Harvard). *Price 50 cents.*

XI. **Rudimentary Society among Boys.** By JOHN JOHNSON, A. B. (J. H. U.). *Price 50 cents.*

XII. **Land Laws of Mining Districts.** By CHARLES HOWARD SHINN, A. B. (J. H. U.); Editor of the *Overland Monthly.* *Price 50 cents.*

FIRST SERIES.—Local Institutions.—1883.

I. **An Introduction to American Institutional History.** By Professor EDWARD A. FREEMAN. With an account of Mr. Freeman's Visit to Baltimore, by the Editor. *Price 25 cents.*

II. **The Germanic Origin of New England Towns.** By H. B. ADAMS. With Notes on Co-operation in University Work. *Price 50 cents.*

III. **Local Government in Illinois.** By ALBERT SHAW, Ph. D. (J. H. U.). —**Local Government in Pennsylvania.** By E. R. L. GOULD, Ph. D. (J. H. U.). *Price 30 cents.*

IV. **Saxon Tithingmen in America.** By H. B. ADAMS. *Price 50 cents.*

V. **Local Government in Michigan, and the Northwest.** By E. W. BEMIS, Ph. D. (J. H. U.). *Price 25 cents.*

VI. **Parish Institutions of Maryland.** By EDWARD INGLE, A. B. (J. H. U.). *Price 40 cents.*

VII. **Old Maryland Manors.** By JOHN JOHNSON, A. B. (J. H. U.) *Price 30 cents.*

VIII. **Norman Constables in America.** By H. B. ADAMS. *Price 50 cents.*

IX-X. **Village Communities of Cape Ann and Salem.** By H. B. ADAMS.

XI. **The Genesis of a New England State (Connecticut).** By Professor ALEXANDER JOHNSTON (Princeton). *Price 30 cents.*

XII. **Local Government and Free Schools in South Carolina.** By B. J. RAMAGE, Ph. D. (J. H. U.). *Price 40 cents.*

JOHNS HOPKINS UNIVERSITY STUDIES

IN

Historical and Political Science.

HERBERT B. ADAMS, Editor.

The first annual series of monthly monographs devoted to History, Politics, and Economics was begun in 1882–3. Four volumes have thus far appeared.

A library edition of the entire set of four volumes, indexed and bound in olive-green cloth, is now ready. Price $12.50 net.

Separate volumes bound in black or olive-green cloth will be sold as follows:

VOLUME I.—Local Institutions. 479 pp. $4.00.

VOLUME II.—Institutions and Economics. 629 pp. $4.00.

VOLUME III.—Maryland, Virginia, and Washington. 595 pp. $4.00.

VOLUME IV.—Municipal Government and Land Tenure. 600 pp. $3.50.

VOLUME V.—Municipal Government and Economics. (*In progress.*)

This Volume, the Fifth Series (1887), *will be furnished in monthly parts upon receipt of subscription price,* $3.

All communications relating to subscriptions, exchanges, etc., should be addressed to the PUBLICATION AGENCY (N. MURRAY), JOHNS HOPKINS UNIVERSITY, BALTIMORE, MARYLAND. Subscriptions will also be received, or single copies furnished by any of the following

AMERICAN AGENTS:

New York.—G. P. Putnam's Sons, 27 and 29 West 23d St.

New Haven.—E. P. Judd, Chapel St.

Boston. — Damrell & Upham (Old Corner Book-Store).

Providence.—Tibbitts & Preston.

Philadelphia.—Porter & Coates.

Montreal.—Dawson Brothers.

Washington. — W. H. Lowdermilk & Co.

Baltimore.—John Murphy & Co.; Cushings & Bailey.

Cincinnati.—Robert Clarke & Co.

Chicago.—A. C. McClurg & Co.

St. Louis.—C. H. Evans & Co.

Louisville.—John P. Morton & Co.

EUROPEAN AGENTS:

London.—Trübner & Co.; or G. P. Putnam's Sons.

Paris.—A. Hermann, 8 Rue de la Sorbonne; Em. Terquem, 15 Boulevard St. Martin.

Strassburg.—Karl J. Trübner.

Berlin.—Puttkammer & Mühlbrecht; Mayer & Müller.

Leipzig.—F. A. Brockhaus.

Turin, Florence, and Rome,—E. Loescher.